Murdo

Murdo

MARGOT SPEIGHT

pictures by
Bill Belcher

COLLINS

William Collins Sons & Co Ltd

London · Glasgow · Sydney

Auckland · Toronto · Johannesburg

First published 1983

ISBN 0 00 184528 4

Printed in Great Britain by
Richard Clay (The Chaucer Press) Ltd,
Bungay, Suffolk

For
David Speight
and
Sam Jowers

My name is Graham.

This is my friend Murdo. It is quite warm standing next to him. He is actually fairly harmless, unless you annoy him.

This is how we first met. I heard a funny noise at the back door and when I opened it I got a shock. There was Murdo. When he snorted at me, his breath melted my Wellington boots which I had left outside on the step. I was going to slam the door in his face, but then I noticed that he was crying. Big tears were rolling down his nose and turning to steam. I began to feel not quite so scared, and in fact to be sorry for him – he was so ugly.

As I stood staring at him, he sighed, scorching the handle of the stiff broom that leaned against the wall of the back yard.

"What's the matter, then?" I said, and got up enough

courage to touch his ear sympathetically. He rolled his eyes at me. He could tell I meant to be kind. "Lost your treasure, have you?" I went on, because I knew that dragons were supposed to care a lot about the treasures they guarded in ancient times; but I didn't know if they still bothered to do it. "I'll help you find a new treasure," I said.

He lumbered nearer to me and laid his big ugly head on my foot, burning it a bit. I realized that we were going to be friends. But I had nowhere to put him, until I remembered the shed I kept my bike in at the end of our yard. My mother never opened the shed door because she was afraid of spiders; so I cleared a space in it for Murdo and kept him there. I didn't tell my mother about Murdo, of course. I knew she wouldn't like him.

I got the name Murdo out of a science fiction book. As he is rather slow-witted, he doesn't always remember his name. But then, he has only had it since he met me, and perhaps his real name is something quite different.

I found that he likes to eat potatoes; he just gives them a good scorch and gobbles them whole in their jackets. He can toast his own bread and grill chops and sausages. He loves ice-cream, but has to eat it very quickly before it melts.

Murdo does tricks too, such as getting the caps off milk bottles. He scratches them off with his claws, flicks them into the air, and melts them with a flash of his breath before they hit the ground. Then he drinks the milk. When he first did this, he would wait until the milkman had gone, then creep out of the shed and sneak round all the doorsteps drinking the milk. I was afraid this would make him un-

popular when people found out who was doing it, and although I had got very fond of Murdo I tried to be angry with him. I shouted: "Stop it, Murdo," and frowned fiercely, and he whimpered and crouched at my feet, even though he is bigger than me. I could see that it was no good; he really didn't understand what the matter was. I couldn't chain him up; he would have melted the chain. He had already ruined the bolt on the shed door. But eventually he stopped stealing the milk when he saw that I didn't like it. Dogs are scared of him; he shoots a jet of flame at them and they zoom off up the road. But cats don't mind him; they sit on him to enjoy the warmth.

For the first month that I had Murdo, it was great fun to dash home from school in the afternoons, open the shed door, and say: "Hello, Murdo." He would scramble towards me eagerly with his jaws gaping in a smile. I fed him on scraps from the kitchen, I smuggled bits of meat and sausages off my own plate for him, and every week I spent my pocket money on tins of pet food. He would sleep quietly all day; but after tea, as soon as it was dark, I would take him for a walk along the empty streets.

But I soon began to worry because I could see that he hated not having a treasure. I often lay awake at night wondering what to do, and could not concentrate on my lessons at school. So after a while I started to make him a treasure. I strung hundreds of corks and bottle caps together; I got my mother's beads, old shoes, Christmas decorations, and some bricks, and sprayed them all gold. I put them in a plastic shopping bag and took it down to the shed. I poured them all out of the bag into the corner. Murdo sighed, dutifully climbed on to the pile, and sat on it. He went on guarding it because he knew it pleased me; but the treasure was only an imitation, and he was still not really happy. He crouched in the darkness of the shed, sighing little puffs of steam and perhaps remembering the real treasure hoard he had once guarded and which he had lost. As the days passed, his scales seemed to grow dull, and although he always greeted me with glowing eyes, his head hung lower, and once or twice I noticed tears falling down his snout. I knew that soon I would have to find something really interesting for him to do.

I was so anxious about Murdo that I got into the habit of hurrying home from school to see him so that he wouldn't feel lonely. I used to sit with him while I was doing my homework. Sometimes my teachers asked me why my exercise books always seemed to have scorch marks on them. One of my essays even had a hole burned through it, and the English teacher wrote a note in the margin asking me if I had taken up smoking.

One day in the middle of the Spring term, I came home from school and found that my mother had locked the door and gone shopping without leaving me a key. I would have to wait until she came home. As usual, I went down the yard to the shed to look in on Murdo. He was sitting on his heap of imitation treasure and his eyes glowed affectionately at me like a couple of traffic lights. Snaking out his long neck, he picked up a gold-painted padlock in his jaws and dropped it at my feet.

"Thank you, Murdo," I said.

But he hadn't finished. He took a breath and blasted the padlock into a pool of red-hot metal.

"Be careful, Murdo, you'll set this place on fire," I said; and then I had a really good idea. I often get good ideas, and now I had thought of a way to cheer him up. "Come on, Murdo," I shouted, "come and help me," and he lolloped after me to the house. I got him to blow a flame at the door lock, and it sizzled and fell out of the door. Murdo grinned at me, very pleased with himself.

I let him into the kitchen and gave him some milk, being careful not to let him burn anything. But just as he finished drinking it, I heard my mother coming back. I dragged him upstairs and hid him as well as I could under my bed on a pile of comics. He made a terrific hump under the bed. I got a tooth mug out of the bathroom, and poured water over the comics so they wouldn't burn, and then I dashed down again.

My mother thumped her shopping bags down on the kitchen table and said in a mad voice, "What on earth have you done to the back door lock, Graham? Where do you think we are going to find the money to mend it?" My mother was widowed when my father was killed a few years ago. He had been working on the dockside in our town, and a crane fell on him. Now my mother never had any money to spare. No wonder she was always anxious and unhappy. I felt very sorry about the lock, but I couldn't tell her that

Murdo had done it, could I? I felt my ears turn purple.

"What a nuisance you are," she said, and sat down to take off her shoes. I filled the kettle with water and lit the stove. I thought if I gave her a cup of tea, it might be easier to explain things to her.

"That's a funny smell," she said after a few minutes. "Maybe I left the iron switched on."

"Oh, I'm sure it's not that," I said. "It's probably the smell blowing over from the brewery." I was beginning to smell something funny myself. I measured some tea leaves into the pot, and said, "I'll just make sure." Then I rushed upstairs.

Smoke was pouring out of my bedroom. I ran into the bathroom and got the tooth mug, filled it with water, rushed back into the bedroom, and threw the water on to the comics. Murdo was sitting on them under my bed and they were blazing away nicely. I flew backwards and forwards with the tooth mug between the bedroom and the bathroom; then I heard my mother screaming from behind me in the bedroom doorway. Through the smoke she had caught sight of Murdo's tail sticking out across the floor, and the gigantic hump he made under the mattress.

"Graham," she screamed, "get that thing out of the house. Just look what it's done. There's a hole in your bed. The carpet is ruined. The wallpaper is on fire," and she went on like that. Murdo was terrified. He wriggled out from under the bed and whizzed past her down the stairs, and after pouring a last mugful of water on the fire I went after him.

We were halfway across the yard when I heard my mother shout from the bathroom window, "What is that animal, anyway?"

"It's a dragon," I replied. "I've been keeping him in the shed."

"Well, don't come back here with it," she yelled. "I don't want to see you with it in this house ever again," and she burst out crying.

I ran after Murdo, and found him in the shed trying to hide behind my bike. Then I heard a fire engine approaching. One of our neighbours had seen smoke coming out of the upstairs windows and had telephoned the fire brigade. I led Murdo into the lane behind the house. When I peered round the corner, I saw the firemen jumping out of the engine waving their axes, and I was worried that if they caught Murdo they would chop him to bits. I saw my mother standing in the street sobbing her heart out; then the woman next door came and led her away. While the firemen poured gallons of water into our house, I sat down and cried too, and stroked Murdo's head. We hid behind some dustbins until it was dark.

As we waited for darkness, I took some paper from my school satchel and wrote a letter to my mother.

"Dear Mum," I wrote, "I am sorry about the fire. Murdo and I will go far away and not come back, as we have caused so much trouble. I am going to try and make it up to you for the damage, also pay for the lock on the door. You really would like Murdo a lot if you got to know him. Please forgive us. Yours faithfully, Graham."

I stuck the letter on a nail on the gate. Without thinking about where we would go, we started to walk. I plodded along the dark, silent roads, and Murdo shuffled and slithered along beside me. Sometimes I cried hopelessly as I walked, and sometimes I tried to think what to do next.

Then I realized that we were heading for the river and the docks, where the lights were shining on the cargo ships. When he was alive my father often used to take me there to see the ships he worked on, and now a funny sort of hope began to grow in my mind. I stopped crying, because I knew that very soon I was going to get another good idea.

We went on walking until we reached the streets of warehouses near the river. Some of them were derelict, and there were rows of houses which had been boarded up. We saw nobody about; whenever we heard footsteps we ducked behind a parked lorry. At last we found a yard full of broken machinery and old cars, and we slept there for the rest of the night and most of the next day. We got very hungry, and I huddled against Murdo for warmth.

At last, towards evening, I couldn't stand being hungry any longer. I went out to look for food. There was a small corner shop nearby, but it was closed, and anyway I had no money. Presently I came to a little café on the dockside. The waitress was very kind to me; she gave me some unsold sandwiches, and in return I washed a lot of dishes and dried the glasses for her.

The waitress told me, as I stood at the sink behind the counter, that there was a cargo ship in the dock getting ready to sail for Canada in the morning. It was already loaded, but the captain had delayed the voyage because the shipping company were sending him six passengers. One was a scientist who wanted to observe icebergs in a part of the North Atlantic where ice drifted south from the Arctic seas. The other five were his assistants. The waitress had heard all this from some of the ship's crew who were drinking tea in the café.

This gave me my next good idea. I had heard a lot about Canada at school. Murdo and I would stow away on the ship and begin a new life in that great country. We would make lots of money, and pay my mother for the damage to the

house, and there would be money left over for Murdo to have a real treasure. I hurried back to the scrap metal yard to fetch Murdo.

When we reached the dock fence, Murdo melted the padlocked chain on the gate, and we went on to the dock-side. Under the glaring lights, the ship loomed above us like a wall, black and rusty, and stained with grime. The ship's generators hummed. Her name was written high up on her bows: *Northumbrian Trader*. A gangway led up to the main deck, where a man was banging something with a hammer. Luckily he had his back to us, and we started to climb up the gangway. The planks sagged and creaked under Murdo's weight, and every moment I expected the seaman to turn round and catch us. Murdo halted in a sudden panic, but I dragged and pushed him on board. Then we crept (or at least I did: Murdo slithered, his claws scraping horribly loud) to a door. I used to go on ships with my father so I knew that there should be stairs going down to the holds and the engine room. Perhaps we would find somewhere down there to hide.

Sure enough, the door opened on to a stairway. We hurried down it, and then down another flight of stairs, then along a corridor. Here was a door marked ENGINE ROOM – KEEP OUT. It opened on to a metal balcony, and below was a huge deep room full of machinery, dials, pipes, catwalks, and ladders, all shining with grease. Behind a small door marked STORES was a small room like a cubby-hole, with a lot of mops and buckets and pipes. This would be a good place for a dragon.

At that moment footsteps rang on the iron ladders below; somebody was coming up to the balcony. I grabbed Murdo and we squeezed together into the storeroom. The footsteps passed our door, and I drew a deep breath. Then I discovered that Murdo, in his agitation, had burnt two holes in my pullover. There really wasn't going to be space for both of us in there. Presently he grew calmer, and curled up under the pipes. He was worn out with all the excitement, and seemed about to go to sleep, so I left him with a ham sandwich, and closed the door gently. He would be fairly safe in the storeroom, there was nothing in it he could set on fire.

Now I had to think about where to hide myself. I peered cautiously over the balcony railing down into the engine room, but it didn't look much use to me. I decided to go on deck again. As I reached the top of the stairs, a man in a cook's hat went past the outside doorway without seeing me. Farther along the main deck I found the companion way, a steep ladder leading to the boatdeck and the bridge above. I dodged along the boatdeck to where a lifeboat rested in a frame, lashed down with ropes. I pulled up the edge of the tarpaulin boat-cover, crawled under it as fast as I could, and fell into the darkness inside.

My first night in the lifeboat wasn't too bad. It was very draughty and cold, but the cover kept out the rain, and I used a canvas bag as a pillow. In spite of not being able to stop shivering, I managed to get some sleep. But just before dawn I was woken by the sound of heavy boots clumping up the gangway from the dockside.

I peeped through a hole in the tarpaulin and saw five men boarding the ship. These must be the passengers. Their bags

seemed surprisingly awkward and heavy to carry. A junior officer, who I later found out was called Mr Pumpkinshaw, ran down from the bridge to greet them and take them to their cabins, but they hardly bothered to speak to him. They were surly and scowling, and looked more like jailbirds than a scientist's assistants. A seaman followed them carrying some more luggage; one of the suitcases had "Professor S. Shadow" printed on its side in black letters. Professor Shadow must be the sixth passenger, the scientist, but I fell asleep again and so I did not see him come on board. An hour later I was woken by the throbbing of engines and the steady heaving and rolling of the ship. We were at sea.

Through my peephole I saw a grey sky and big waves bearded with foam. I was still shivering, and could not feel my hands or feet. The sea was rough, and I kept getting thrown about inside the lifeboat as the ship rode up the sides of the steep waves, dived over their backs, and rolled in the troughs between them. Even the seamen were staggering as they walked across the slippery decks and climbed up and down the ladders. Showers of icy spray blew over us, and the cold, hard wind found its way into every corner of my hiding place, and went straight through my pullover and jacket. Once or twice I crept down to Murdo's room and got warm by squashing myself in beside him where he lay snoozing. The rocking of the ship was making him sleepier than usual, but I could not sleep. I kept thinking about food. We had eaten all our sandwiches.

On the second day I waited until the Cook went on to the bridge to take the Captain a cup of tea; then I scurried into the empty galley and rummaged in the waste-bin. I found a lot of left-over bread, bacon rinds, and apple cores, stuffed them into my pockets, and dashed back to Murdo. On the third day I did the same thing again, and although we were still hungry, this food was better than nothing.

On the fourth day, however, just as I was putting a half-eaten lamb chop up my shirt, the Cook caught me. He dragged me up to the chartroom on the bridge to show me to the Captain.

Captain Rumbold was a stout man with a red face, and he sat at his chart-table writing in his logbook. Beside him stood a younger officer, and in an armchair by the window sat a bright-eyed elderly man, leaning forward on a carved black stick. I could tell he was Professor Shadow.

"I found this boy stowing away, sir," said the Cook, gripping me by the collar. "Stand up straight, boy, and show Captain Rumbold that chop."

I told the Captain about my mother, and that I had burned our house down, and had run away to find work so that I could get money for her; I explained that I was very hungry and had not meant to steal anything except what was to be thrown away, and I said I would be glad to make myself useful during the voyage.

Captain Rumbold was angry, but he understood my point of view. Instead of clapping me in irons, as he said he would at first, he just gave me a good telling-off and a promise of work.

"You can start by cleaning out the bilges," he said, his eyebrows bristling and his nose red with annoyance. "Our

Mr Dunkem here is the First Mate, and you will obey any orders he gives you. When you have done the bilges, you can give the Cook a hand in the galley at dinner-time." I thanked him, and as I meekly followed the Cook out of the cabin, I wondered what the Captain would say if he knew that he had a dragon on his ship.

That evening we ran into a storm. I was impressed by the way that most of the crew went on bravely working, even on deck where the huge waves threatened them. But the Professor's five assistants seemed nervous; the Cook said he had overheard them saying the Captain was an old fool and that he would shipwreck us, steering us into bad weather like this. I was scared myself – after all, it was my first voyage – but like the crew I trusted Captain Rumbold to get us safely through the storm.

All the same, I found that cleaning out the bilges, where the grimy, oily water washed around in the bottom of the ship, was not much fun. There were greasy smells, and the rolling of the ship made me sick and dizzy. Poor Murdo was also quite ill. He wriggled farther and farther under the nest of pipes and cables, moaning and hardly able to raise a puff of steam.

I asked the Cook to give me some pills for seasickness and Murdo swallowed them. They stopped him from being sick, but they made him drowsy, and he took no interest in the odds and ends of food I brought him. It was lucky in a way that he was so sleepy. I had enough to do to keep up with my work, let alone look after him. When I had finished mopping up the bilge water, I peeled potatoes for the Cook and ran up to the bridge with cups of tea for the Captain or Mr Dunkem.

Then I had to keep rushing down to the storeroom to see to Murdo, making sure that nobody observed me. But it was going to be much worse when the weather improved and Murdo felt like stretching his legs.

But the weather didn't get better. Instead it got wilder and wilder. Enormous mountains of solid grey water crashed over us, and we had to cling to things, or crawl on the floors, to get about the ship. Nobody was allowed on deck for fear they would get swept away. Down in the bilges I could hear the waves hammering at the thick steel plates of the hull only inches away from me, and when a wave smashed the lifeboat I had hidden in, I was glad of the small, uncomfortable bunk I had been given in the carpenter's workshop. On winter nights I had often listened anxiously to the wind and rain beating on my bedroom window, and wondered what a storm at sea was like. Now I knew.

The storm went on for days. Then one morning the sea was calm at last; the ship rolled in the swell, buried in fog, her foghorn booming out every few seconds. As I helped the Cook clear up the broken crockery in the galley, he told me about other awful storms he had been in, and I hoped that after we reached Canada I would never have to go to sea again. But Canada was still a long way off.

The fog pressed round the ship, dense and silent. The Cook and I made sandwiches, and when I carried the tray up to the wheelhouse on the bridge, the fog wrapped itself over me as damp and close as a wet blanket. The officers on watch were continually scanning the radar screens. Professor Shadow was in the wheelhouse too, peering at the fog, and sometimes looking at the compass. We were far to the north now, heading westwards for the port of Halifax on the Canadian coast, nearly two thousand miles away. We had already come hundreds of miles farther than I had ever been in my whole life before. The ship was moving very slowly, and I was impatient. I wanted to get to Canada as soon as possible.

Mr Dunkem, biting crossly into his cheese and pickle sandwich, told me not to be in such a hurry. The ship had to proceed with caution because a danger far greater than the storm lay ahead of us. Icebergs! We were near the Arctic currents which carried them south in the spring, and the fog hid them from us. Even as we stared into the clammy whiteness, we began to hear small chunks of ice knocking and scraping along the sides of the ship, and not far away there was a low growling as sheets of ice in the sea grated against each other. The seaman standing at the wheel kept his eye on the compass, and the engines moved us forward at dead-slow speed.

After a while I carried the tray back down to the main deck, and was leaning over the rail pretending to throw the uneaten crusts to the birds (actually I was stuffing them into my pockets for Murdo) when suddenly there was a terrific jolt and the ship stopped. I staggered and clutched the rail. We had hit a slab of submerged ice. The deck hands working

on the storm-damaged hatches nearby dropped their tools and ran to get their lifejackets. I ran too, towards the stairs leading to Murdo's storeroom. My only thought was to find enough lifejackets to keep him afloat. I met Mr Pumpkinshaw at the foot of the stairs; as I ran past he grabbed me and shouted: "We've sprung a leak!"

He led me to the engine room. Water was welling through a huge crack in one of the steel plates of the hull. The seamen were frantically trying to plug it. A new plate would have to be welded over the hole. The water was already ankle-deep in the engine room; if it rose much higher, the furnaces would be in danger of exploding.

Suddenly I decided I was not going to keep Murdo a secret any longer. I ran along the catwalk to Murdo's room and woke him up. The men, struggling to get the new steel plate into position, were too busy to notice us as we waded over the engine room floor. Murdo seemed to know at once what was needed. Nudging the startled men aside, he sent a jet of white-hot flame round the edges of the plate, sealing it neatly over the crack. The water stopped flooding in.

"Well, I'll be blowed," said the First Engineer, wiping his face with an oily rag. "I haven't seen one of those before. Can he get rid of the water as well?"

"Oh yes," I replied, "but it'll make a lot of steam."

The First Engineer said he didn't care; so Murdo started blowing fire around, and in a few minutes the engine room was free of water, although it looked like our kitchen on washday. The Captain came down in his pyjamas to watch, accompanied by Professor Shadow and some of his assistants.

"Your dragon is quite amazing, Graham," said the Professor. "Would you consider selling him?"

I was shocked. It was clear that the Professor had an unpleasant attitude towards animals. I stood up straight and said, "Murdo is my friend. I'd never sell him. He's only helping here because I asked him to."

"Very nice of him," said the old man. I felt my fingers scorch; it was Murdo licking them. I patted his head and said, "Don't worry, I'll never sell you, Murdo." The Professor smiled at his men in what I thought was rather an odd way.

The Trader's crew, who had all crowded into the engine room, cheered Murdo three times, and the Cook gave him a big bucket full of ice-cream. As I held the bucket for Murdo to lick out, the Captain said, "Seeing he has been such a help, that dragon can stay. Graham, make sure that he behaves himself and doesn't set the ship on fire."

I saluted the Captain gratefully and replied, "Aye, aye, sir," and the crew cheered again. But the Professor and his assistants did not join in; they were not happy about Murdo joining the ship's company.

After I had taken Murdo back to his quarters, I returned to the engine room to wipe up the puddles on the floor. The Trader's engines started up again, and she carried on ploughing slowly through the icy sea. The fog continued to blot out everything beyond a few yards, and its sinister whiteness was penetrated only by the foghorn. Our troubles were just beginning, had we but known it.

An hour later, I was wringing out the cloth I had been using, and was thinking of going back to the galley sink, when the ship gave a great lurch, and stopped once again. I and all my crew mates were thrown off our feet. Mr Dunkem's voice came down from the bridge through the loudspeaker: "We are trapped in an icefloe. It looks as if we are going to be frozen in completely. All hands on deck!"

We did not need to be told twice: we swarmed up the

ladders and out on deck. We tried pouring hot water on to the menacing ice, but it clung to us, thicker and stronger by the minute. The engines were not powerful enough to force the ship free, and she began to drift helplessly. We attacked the ice with pickaxes, but as fast as we got rid of it more ice formed. We stared despairingly into the fog; all we could see was the ice-pack's bumpy crust.

The Cook said in a joking way, "We'll be here till Christmas." It wasn't very funny. Nobody laughed. We were thinking that we would never get to Canada; I was wondering if I would ever see my mother again.

The Professor had been watching our efforts with a faint smile. He popped another sugar lump into the tea I had brought him, while the Captain glared through the bridge windows and let his tea get cold.

"Perhaps Murdo can find a way out," suggested the Professor.

"Yes," said the Captain, brightening up. "What about that dragon?"

I fetched Murdo on deck and made him lean over the bows. I pointed to the thick layers of ice below us.

"Blow, Murdo, blow," I said to him. He stretched out his neck and puffed sheets of flame at the frozen slabs which lay in our way. They started to melt. Murdo puffed away for an hour; then the Trader began to inch forward into the fog. We were free!

The Trader plodded on through the ice-pack at dead-slow speed, and it was nightfall before we were clear of it. We soon gave up trying to see anything in the fog and darkness.

Next morning, however, a light wind came up, a hazy sun appeared, and the fog lifted. I went on to the bridge to clear away the tea mugs, and found Mr Dunkem staring at something through his binoculars.

"How did that get there?" he said.

I looked through the binoculars at the horizon, and saw what seemed to be a distant bank of clouds.

"It's an island where there isn't supposed to be one," said Mr Dunkem. "It's not on the chart. We're lost."

"The pack-ice carried us off course," roared the Captain. "You should have corrected our position, Dunkem."

Professor Shadow was very busy looking at the island through his binoculars and jotting down notes in a little book. His pencil trembled.

He turned to Captain Rumbold, "This island is not marked on your chart, Captain, for the good reason that it has remained undiscovered until this moment. But I knew, from my extensive researches, that I would find it somewhere round here. Now I have the chance to prove another of my theories correct. It is of the greatest scientific importance that we go ashore."

"Is it dangerous?" asked Mr Dunkem. "Maybe we should take Murdo with us, just in case."

"Dangerous? Rubbish, Dunkem," snorted the Captain. "You heard the Professor. Get a boat ready and go ashore."

The Professor looked very pleased.

"Well, yes," the Captain added, "you might as well take that animal along – and Graham had better go too, to take care of him."

The Professor's smile faded somewhat.

"You'll be going, naturally, Professor," said Captain Rumbold hastily. "You'll be seeing to the scientific part of it."

I fetched Murdo from his room. The Professor borrowed an oilskin coat and got his stick. Mr Dunkem picked half a dozen of his men and they lowered a lifeboat over the side. Meanwhile the radio officer tried to get in touch with the shipping company to tell them about the island. The Captain and Mr Pumpkinshaw stayed on the bridge to work out our position with their instruments.

Mr Dunkem and I and the Professor and the six seamen climbed down into the boat, and Murdo, tied up in a cargo net and fuming with annoyance, was lowered on top of us. He made a big fuss and got his claws tangled up, but Mr Dunkem said he would just have to get used to being lifted on and off the ship like this. I gave him a chip butty to keep him quiet. He kept getting his legs and tail stuck under the seats but we pushed and pulled him until we got him sitting amidships. He was tired after mending the cracked steel plate and melting the ice, and now the strain of being loaded into a small boat wore him out completely. We drew the net from under him, and he fell asleep. He managed not to scorch anything for once, his breath only emerging in small clouds of steam. The men who were rowing said they did not mind; it kept their feet warm. They began to pull hard on the oars, and we headed for the island.

It was a beautiful morning, very cold, but with a bright blue sky, and the waves were small and gentle, not like the ones that had battered us during the storm. The island was half-veiled in mist, but as we drew nearer we could see its cliffs crowded with seabirds. The Professor pointed out the curious formations in the rocks, the scars left by glaciers, and the caves and clefts gouged out by the sea.

"It looks just like an iced birthday cake stuck in the middle of nowhere," I remarked to the Professor.

"To me it may be the reward of a lifetime's work," he replied. As I sat beside him, I felt him trembling. He could not wait to go ashore.

We anchored the boat in a small cove, and left Murdo asleep in it. We waded through the shallow water and scrambled up the cliff, with the Professor leading the way.

It was wonderful to be on solid ground again. I looked back from the cliff top to see if Murdo was all right; then we strode inland over the snow. The Professor darted about tapping the rocks with a little hammer, and put some of the smaller ones in his pocket. We asked him a lot of questions, and he answered them in a very friendly way. But all the time he was looking from side to side and running from rock to rock, so that I began to feel uneasy. Under his friendly manner, he was hiding more than anxiety: it was something greedy, perhaps evil. One by one we dropped behind him, and he hurried on alone.

Then as he mounted the shoulder of the hill above us, he stopped suddenly. As I came up behind him, I saw a jutting peak of stone, about fifty feet high, that was crusted with ice. But it wasn't blue and white and glittering, it was brown and yellow with dark stains. In fact, it wasn't ice at all. Professor Shadow ran towards it and prodded it.

"Come and look at this," he shouted.

We all walked over and had a look; it didn't seem very interesting. It was a kind of loose, crumbling rock, like dirty sugar.

"It is quintillium," said Professor Shadow. His voice sounded choked. "It is one of the rarest substances known to science."

"Is it valuable?" I asked.

"Is it valuable?" repeated the Professor, glaring at me through his glasses. Then he smiled. "Only to those who know how to use it." Under his breath he added, "At last!"

"Shall we take a bit back to the ship, sir, to show the

Captain?" asked Mr Dunkem.

With a penknife the Professor scraped a few flakes off one of the dirty-sugar stones and put them in his pocket. Then he told Mr Dunkem to record the exact position of the quintillium by taking a compass-bearing. He glanced at his watch and wrote down the time in his notebook. He could hardly hold his pencil, he was trembling so much.

"We must return to the ship at once," he said. "I shall contact the shipping company on the radio-telephone and tell them about this unique mineral deposit."

"But sir," said Mr Dunkem, "the Captain told us to explore the island."

"Later, later, young man," snapped Professor Shadow, and he hastened back towards the beach. As we turned away from the quintillium to follow him, we saw Murdo coming to meet us, his tongue hanging out. He had woken up to find himself alone, and had come to find us. He slithered towards the Professor.

"Oh good," I said. "Murdo will know if the quintillium is valuable; he can always tell a real treasure."

"Out of my way, you ugly beast," cried the old man. Murdo, wanting to be friendly, tried to lick his hand, but the Professor backed away in a panic and raised his carved stick. To my horror, I saw that it was not an ordinary walking stick, but a swordstick. He had twisted the handle and drawn the blade, and was poking it at Murdo's nose. Murdo stared at it in surprise.

"Keep still, Murdo," I shouted. "It's all right, Professor, he won't hurt you."

"I will skewer him with this swordstick if he so much as bats an eyelid," snarled Professor Shadow. "He's dangerous. He should have been tied up." Murdo retreated a yard or two, alarmed at the angry voice, and swinging his head about.

Then he caught sight of the quintillium. With a tremendous, booming, ear-splitting roar, which terrified all of us because we had never before heard him make such a noise, he rushed towards it, knocking Mr Dunkem and me flying.

The Professor wailed, "Stop him."

I shouted, "Murdo, come here," in a loud, fierce voice. Murdo halted with a snort. I ran up and grabbed him by the spikes on his back. His eyes were glowing green. There was no doubt that the Professor had been right; the quintillium was as valuable as gold, or moon rocks, a perfect dragon's hoard. All Murdo wanted to do was to climb on top of it and guard it. It was obvious that nobody could stop him. But I was afraid that the Professor, rather than let Murdo have the quintillium, would kill him with the swordstick. Even now he was tightening his grip on the handle of the weapon. He would attack before Murdo had time to defend himself.

"Professor," I said, my voice squeaky with fear, "you must let him keep it. He has been looking for a treasure to hoard for ages."

"Never," said Professor Shadow. "A ridiculous idea. He must be got rid of."

"If you want to kill Murdo," I said, "you will have to kill me first. And by the time you have done that he will be sitting on the quintillium ready to shoot flames at you or anyone else who tries to take it from him."

The Professor's face went all green and purple and twisted with rage. He waved the swordstick and came closer. I tried not to think what it must feel like when a swordstick goes through you. I remembered instead my mother not having enough money to get our house repaired. She was probably sitting at the kitchen table this very minute, crying her eyes out because I had left her, and wishing she had not said such unkind things to me. Tears ran down my face at the idea of being killed, because I am not naturally brave. But I would not let the Professor pass me to get at Murdo. The First Mate and the other men were murmuring in sympathy with me.

The Professor did not care what they thought. But he hesitated for a few moments. Then he smiled cunningly, put the blade back in the stick, and said, "Would Murdo object if we removed the quintillium to the ship? He could sit on it in the hold."

He was clearly intending to make use of Murdo instead of killing him. So I picked up a big lump of the quintillium and staggered off with it down the cliff. Murdo quietly followed me, climbed into the boat, and sat amidships on the lump, squashing it into a heap. We started kicking chunks of quintillium off the outcrop until we had enough to fill the boat; then we rowed back to the ship, with Murdo wobbling on top of the load. The Number Three hold was empty, so we loaded the quintillium into it. Mr Dunkem saw that it was spread evenly, and Murdo sat on it. Then some of the crew, with the Professor's men, returned to the island to get more, and soon the hold was filled to the brim. I stood with the Captain and Mr Pumpkinshaw on the main deck and watched.

"I don't see what good it is," grumbled Captain Rumbold, gazing glumly over the edge of the hold. "It looks like a lot of wet gravel to me."

"Don't worry, Captain," said the Professor, behind us. "You will be famous as the great navigator Rumbold, benefactor of mankind."

Captain Rumbold frowned down at Murdo, who was squatting below us in the hold. "How are we going to get that dragon off the cargo when we land? He gets annoyed when anyone goes near it. Beats me how he hasn't set the ship on fire before now."

"I'll put a fire extinguisher near the Number Three hatch, sir," said Mr Pumpkinshaw.

"All right," said the Captain. "And while I think of it, Pumpkinshaw, go and look up quintillium in the dictionary."

7

The next day was calm and sunny, the sea was a sparkling dark blue, and we were bound for Halifax again. After completing my usual tasks in the galley, I went down to the engine room to look at the plate Murdo had welded. He had done a perfect job, and I thought when we reached Canada I might find him work in a ship-repair yard there – that is, if I could ever get him to leave the quintillium. He was curled up on it now, snoring.

At dinner-time, I helped the Cook to serve at the Captain's table. The Professor, sitting beside the Captain, praised me for my prompt action in getting Murdo to mend the damaged bulkhead. He seemed to have forgotten the incident of the swordstick, and talked a lot about Murdo. He said he was going to write an article about dragons for a scientific journal, and was glad to have one as a sentinel for the quintillium.

"He guards it so well," the Professor said, "that he ought to have some ice-cream as a reward."

"Get a bucket," said Captain Rumbold to the Cook. "These dishes are too small. He might eat one by mistake."

"He can have my strawberries as well," said the Professor. He had sprinkled what looked like powdered sugar on to his plateful of strawberries, and now he spooned them on to the ice-cream. I was pleased that he was getting over

his dislike of Murdo; I carried the bucket down to the hold, and Murdo gobbled up the contents. Then, after the Cook and I had washed up and tidied the galley, we had a game of ping-pong in the recreation room.

As we bounced the ball up and down the table, I said: "The Professor says the quintillium is the world's most valuable substance, and it will be very useful to mankind."

"Well," replied the Cook, "that's his opinion. I don't trust him. I think we should dump it over the side."

"But he can't be lying, or Murdo wouldn't be so keen to sit on it. He only likes to sit on really valuable things."

"If it's valuable we could get highjacked," said the Cook.

I hadn't thought of that. "But that's only if some hijackers got to know about it," I said, "and they can't have done, because we've only just found it."

"It's a wicked world," said the Cook. "The Professor was in the radio room all afternoon, sending coded messages to somebody, and you can bet your boots it wasn't the shipping company. I don't like him, and I don't like those shifty fellows of his, whispering to each other when they think nobody's watching them. If you ask me, something rum's going on."

"Don't worry, Cookie," I replied. "Murdo would never let them touch the quintillium. He thinks it's his."

I smiled at the thought of Murdo snoring in the hold; then I suddenly thought of the powder the Professor had sprinkled on the strawberries.

"You're right!" I gasped.

We rushed out on deck and peered down through a hole in the Number Three hold hatch-cover. I called Murdo's name softly. There was no response, no glowing yellow eye shining up at me. Murdo did not move. Only a faint mist of steam came from his nose.

"Doped!" said the Cook. "That wicked old geezer doped the strawberries!" He saw me turn pale, and added, "Don't take on, sonny. It might not be fatal."

"I must tell the Captain," I said grimly, and I ran up the companionway leading to the bridge so fast that I scarcely touched the hand-rail. As my eyes came level with the wheelhouse door, I stopped in horror.

Captain Rumbold, who had come on watch while Mr Dunkem went to bed, was stretched over the table with Professor Shadow's swordstick at his throat. The Captain's eyes were popping out and his nose was purple. Mr Pumpkinshaw cowered in a corner. Trivett, the seaman at the wheel, was trembling so much he could hardly keep his gaze on the compass. I put my hands over my mouth to stop myself shouting.

"Steer due north, my good man," the Professor was saying, "or I'll pin your captain to his own log-book."

There didn't seem to be anything lying about that I could hit him with, and there was nobody to help me. Pumpkinshaw stared hypnotized at the swordstick, and the Cook had stopped on the companionway behind me, too terrified to come further.

"Trivett, you steer this vessel one point off the compass-heading she's on, and I'll skin you alive personally as soon as I get out of this mess," roared the Captain. "No scallywag of a scientist is going to hijack my ship."

For a moment I thought Trivett would obey him; like the rest of the crew he had a lot of respect for the Captain. But slowly he let the wheel come over and I felt the ship heel slightly. We were heading due north.

I thought the Captain would have a fit, he was so angry. I whispered to the Cook, "Go and get some help," and he scurried down to the main deck. Then I coughed loudly, waited a few moments, and walked into the wheelhouse.

"Excuse me, Captain Rumbold," I said, "I've come to report a difficulty in Number Three hold."

The Captain was standing up straightening his tie. The Professor was behind him; he concealed the swordstick from me under the table, and watched Trivett with a nasty smile. I winked at the Captain to show that I knew what was happening.

"I'm busy just now," said the Captain. "What's the trouble?"

"Something's going wrong with the cargo, sir," I said. "It's making funny noises."

The Professor started forward anxiously.

"Perhaps you'd better look at it, Professor," I went on, and walked back to the door, hoping that he would follow me and give the Captain a chance to knock him down.

But the Professor did not stir. He had noticed a movement below on the main deck, and at once guessed that I knew what he was up to and that I had sent for help.

"You're a clever little chap, Graham," he said, "but not quite clever enough. Following my instructions, my men handcuffed the radio officer to his own transmitter as soon as I finished sending messages to my headquarters. By this time they will have also overpowered the Chief Engineer and the rest of the crew. Captain Rumbold, you and Graham and all your men will be put into the lifeboats, and while I take this ship to where I can deal with the quintillium uninterrupted, you will be left at the mercy of the dark and frozen sea to make your way to England."

"What about Murdo?" I asked in a small voice.

The Professor turned on me with a snarl. "If I can't make use of him," he said, "I shall have him hoisted over the side and dropped on an iceberg."

I could not believe it. Tears fell down my cheeks.

Captain Rumbold laid his big red hand on my shoulder. "Now, Graham," he said, "Don't give way. We aren't done for yet. We'll keep watching for our chance."

8

Our chance did not come. With his blade still pointed at the Captain's neck, the Professor forced us to go down to the main deck. Captain Rumbold's face went grey when he saw the crew of the Trader standing there with their hands up. Behind them were the Professor's assistants holding automatic rifles and pistols. No wonder the baggage they had brought with them on board had been so heavy and awkward.

While the Professor was shouting orders to his men, we heard the distant sound of a helicopter engine approaching the ship from the north-east. As it drew nearer, we grew excited, hoping desperately that it was someone coming to our rescue. It circled the ship with chattering rotors, then hovered over our heads. When its door opened and a man leaned out aiming a machine gun at us, the Professor smiled at our disappointment.

"Now, you see," he hissed, "how necessary it is to obey me."

We were loaded into the three undamaged lifeboats. The Cook and I were in the Captain's boat, Mr Dunkem and Mr Pumpkinshaw took charge of the other two. The worst part was leaving the ship that had been our home. We sat in the lifeboats bobbing in the water against the Trader's steep, rusty sides and felt very small. As I crammed myself on to the stern-seat next to Captain Rumbold, I tried not to cry. We were leaving Murdo behind in the hold of the Trader, fast asleep and ignorant of his fate.

The helicopter, still hovering, was letting down a cable into the Number Three hold. The Captain suddenly grabbed me by the arms, just in time, for when I realized what the Professor intended to do next, I almost jumped overboard to swim back to the ship. The cable was winched up, and hanging from the end of it in a net was poor Murdo. They were going to drop him in the sea!

I screamed, "Don't drop him! I don't think he can swim!" But the Professor, who was supervising the operation from the bridge, did not hear me. He wouldn't have listened anyway.

"Quick, boys, pull on your oars. Graham, watch where they let him drop," and the Captain bent down and dragged a big rubber bundle from a locker. A white cord dangled from it, and this he wound round his wrist. The helicopter swung away from the ship in our direction, and Murdo, disturbed by the movement, opened his eyes. Mr Dunkem, at the helm of the boat next to us, yelled at his men to row for their lives, for the helicopter was positioning its load directly above them. The helicopter crew, seeing Mr Dunkem's boat escaping them, hesitated, and seemed to be arguing about whether or not to drop Murdo on us instead.

That hesitation gave us time to get out of the way. Murdo gazed in surprise at the waves beneath him, and at the strange machine above, and let out a white-hot blast of flame. The cable sizzled, then snapped, and the helicopter bounced violently upwards. His tail and wings entangled in the net, Murdo plummeted into the water between our boat and Mr Dunkem's, drenching us with spray. The Captain pulled on the white cord and flung the bundle towards the spot where Murdo had landed; it began to unfold, and now it inflated itself into a life-raft. After a lot of floundering about, and a lot of shouting from me, Murdo broke out of the net, scrambled onto the raft, and stared around. Steam poured off him. He looked properly awake, and very angry. He roared several times, and snorted flames, and the helicopter flew hastily away.

"We must get this animal into one of the boats," Mr Dunkem shouted through his cupped hands above the noise.

"Well, all right, get him into yours," bawled the Captain.

"He's nearer to your boat, sir," yelled Mr Dunkem. "Besides, you've got a fire blanket in your locker, and we haven't."

"Hurry up, you fool, and grab him," shrieked Captain Rumbold. "He's melting the raft; can't you smell it?"

"Not from here, sir," Mr Dunkem yelled back. "Anyway,

you've got hold of the rope on the raft, haven't you?"

I won't tell you what the Captain said next; but it ended up with Murdo getting into our boat and the Cook and me throwing buckets of water over him. The resulting steam made a thick fog round us, but when he calmed down it condensed and collected in the bilges, and we had to keep baling it out. The men rowed; the Captain took his place sitting in the stern with his compass in one hand and the tiller in the other. He grumbled and groaned as he steered the boat into the darkness of the ocean. The other boats kept close to us. The Captain kept turning to shake his fist at the Northumbrian Trader, hoping that the Professor could still see him. But the ship grew smaller and smaller in the widening distance. I watched it over the Captain's shoulder until it disappeared altogether in the night. All I could hear was the splashing of the oars in the water, the hissing of the wave crests as they reared themselves ahead of us, and the occasional complaints of the crew as they heaved on their oars.

Murdo was very upset about losing the quintillium. He sat choking with sobs which shook our boat in the water. The crew grumbled about it; now that all the excitement had died down, they were beginning to realize that they were in an open boat going heaven alone knew where, and perhaps with bad weather ahead. Some of them got downhearted and started sobbing like Murdo. None of us expected to see our families again, or to walk on dry land, or even to survive the bitter Arctic night.

But the Captain looked at the stars and said that the fine weather would hold, and that we were heading for Greenland, more or less. He found a box of useful things in the locker: a radio, a ukelele, biscuits, some jumpers, and a packet of chocolate, which he passed around. He steered the boat with his knee against the tiller, and sang several songs, accompanying himself on the ukelele. We all cheered up and sang, and Murdo kept us warm. We took turns sleeping and rowing, and so, in spite of our desperate situation, we felt brave and full of hope.

But when the sun rose the next morning on the empty sea, once more our spirits fell. Apart from our three boats, there was no sign of any other ships. Eventually Captain Rumbold switched on the radio and twiddled the knobs. After some static noises, an announcer's voice said: "Spotter planes from the air forces of six nations are hunting the missing crew of the merchant vessel Northumbrian Trader, bound for Halifax, and discovered early this morning abandoned among icebergs to the north-west of Iceland. The crew abandoned ship in such a hurry that the Cook left a beef stew burning on the galley stove."

"That was going to be today's dinner," sighed the Cook. "I knew I had forgotten something."

"Reports that the ship may have been carrying a hazardous cargo were denied by the shipping company's owners, who said that she was loaded only with frozen strawberries and transistor radios, and that the Number Three hold was empty. No radio signals have been received from the Northumbrian Trader since the day before yesterday when her radio officer made a routine weather check with Icelandic coastguards. She had been blown off course after a collision with an iceberg. The distinguished scientist Professor Sigismund Shadow who was a passenger is among the missing. Rescue services fear it may soon be necessary to give up the search for survivors . . ."

The men had stopped rowing, and we were sitting still, listening to the broadcast. When we heard the last words we all gave a yell of fright. "Quiet!" shouted the Captain, and the announcer went on: ". . . wreckage of a rubber life-raft identified as belonging to the Northumbrian Trader. Now here are the football results. . . ."

We began arguing fiercely. The Captain waved to Mr Dunkem and Mr Pumpkinshaw to bring their boats alongside. Their crews were all quarrelling and grumbling like us. There was a discussion about what to do.

The Captain said that we were still four hundred miles from Greenland, and it would take us more than a week to get there, even if the good weather continued. Our best chance for survival was to get into one of the regular shipping routes and hope that someone spotted us.

Mr Pumpkinshaw said, "But where can the Professor have got to, with the Trader lying abandoned and the Number Three hold empty? He must have unloaded the quintillium somewhere, and left the ship to drift. But then where would he go?"

We argued about it for a while, and at last there was a despairing silence.

Then Murdo sat up and smiled at us, refreshed from his long rest. Some of the men leaned over from the other boats to pat his head and warm their hands on his scaly body. He puffed steam gently over them. A man in Mr Dunkem's boat offered him a biscuit.

"Put that biscuit away," snapped the Captain. "We haven't got enough food for ourselves, never mind giving it to dragons."

"He's hungry, sir," said the man, reluctantly putting the biscuit back in the tin. Murdo snorted with disappointment, and started stretching towards the tin, scrambling and slithering over the gunwhale, and nearly tipping our boat over.

"Get hold of his tail," shouted the Captain. Two men grabbed Murdo by the tail, and he struggled and flapped his wings. They had been folded up most of the time; in fact, they usually were, and I had never seen him use them. But now they were waving like giant umbrellas blown inside out. Our boat spun round in the wind from them. It suddenly dawned on me that he might be good at flying.

"Captain Rumbold," I cried, "I've got a wonderful idea."

"About time," growled the Captain. "This boat is turning into a corkscrew. And that ass Dunkem is laughing his head off. Graham, if you don't control that dragon, he'll have the lot of us at the bottom of the sea before you can say Jack Robinson."

I managed to calm Murdo down long enough to get some ropes round his back legs. The crew helped me make these fast to the bow-lines of the boats. I tied two steering ropes to Murdo's ears. Then I fed him a handful of biscuits from our emergency supply, pointed his head to the south-west by the Captain's compass, and shouted: "Hold tight, everybody!"

It took Murdo several minutes to get used to this new arrangement. Presently, thinking it must be some sort of game, he began to enjoy it. He flapped his wings in earnest, then suddenly took off and went like the wind. The boats scooted over the water with all of us hanging on for dear life. The violent jerk of the bow-lines caused Mr Dunkem to fall over backwards, with his legs kicking in the air in the bottom of the boat. The Cook was so scared he put his hands over his eyes. The Captain, using some shocking language, took me by the scruff of my neck and stuffed me under his seat out of harm's way. Then he started baling water out of the boat as fast as he could go. Murdo, looking like a tent that had got loose in a gale, flapped along happily, his tongue hanging out.

All of a sudden the men were shouting and pointing at the compass.

"Where does that son of a demented egg-beater think he's going?" said Captain Rumbold. "He's altered course for the north-east."

"He's probably picked up the scent of the quintillium," I yelled from under the stern-seat.

Captain Rumbold tugged furiously at the ropes attached to Murdo's ears, but it was useless. Murdo ignored him.

"Let him follow the scent, Captain," I said. "He's sure to find it, and find Professor Shadow too, so that he can be brought to justice. And we might get rescued on the way."

This last idea seemed to appeal to Captain Rumbold. He gave Murdo his head, and in a few hours we were back where we had started – where Professor Shadow had first cast us adrift. The spotter planes, however, were nowhere to be seen; they must have been searching in a fresh area, or perhaps they had given up the search altogether. Murdo whirled us round two or three times, apparently wondering where the ship had gone. Then, growling, he headed north. I could see that no matter where the Professor had taken the quintillium, Murdo would be sure to find him.

We stopped while Murdo rested, and we ate our rations. Then we sped onwards until nearly sunset. Just as the sun was dipping into the sea, the Cook gave a yell and pointed.

"A ship!"

There was a small cargo ship, silhouetted on the red horizon. While the Captain was fumbling with his binoculars, Mr Dunkem whipped out a knife.

"I will cut my boat loose and go for help," he shouted, and before anyone could stop him, he had cut the bow-line of his boat that was fastened to Murdo's foot and steered away for the tanker, his men heaving on their oars.

"Just a minute," shouted the Captain. "Come back here." But Mr Dunkem was already out of earshot, for with one less boat to pull, Murdo had increased his speed. It was not long before Mr Dunkem's boat was a mere dot on the waves behind us.

Jamming his hat down over his ears to stop it blowing away, the Captain said, "When we sailed I thought it was going to be a nice, peaceful voyage, and look what happens. I'm too old for this sort of thing. I was hoping to retire next year, but the company will probably reduce my pension for making such a mess of this trip." He grew very gloomy.

"Captain Rumbold," I said, patting his shoulder, "the company ought to have known better than let the Professor on board the Trader. It isn't your fault. If it wasn't for you, we would all be dead now. We will stand by you."

"The best skipper we ever sailed with," said the Cook, and the men all said, "Aye aye."

Captain Rumbold was very touched by our loyalty, and blew his nose several times. "I'm a widower," he said, "and my ship and my men are the nearest thing I have to a home and family. Thank you." He handed out chocolate and a swig of rum to each of us, and although we were still in great danger, we sang songs as we rushed over the waves. We knew that no matter what storms and disasters lay in wait for us, now we were all shipmates together, and it made us feel braver.

11

At dawn, we found ourselves once more among the icebergs. But Murdo had enough sense to keep clear of them, except for bumping us over the odd icefloe. We had long since passed the island where we found the quintillium. We were exhausted by this time, and had tied ourselves into our places, for our hands were too frozen to hold on with. During the night, some of the men had fallen asleep, wedging themselves under their seats so as not to get jolted overboard.

Then the Cook startled us with a cry of: "Land! Land ho!"

"That's not land," said the Captain, rubbing his bleary eyes. "That's a huge iceberg."

"There is a building on it, sir," called Mr Pumpkinshaw. He was standing up in the bows of his boat with his binoculars to his eyes. He took another look and added, "I can see some people too."

We were soon close enough to see that the people were Professor Shadow and his men. They were moving in and out of the building, carrying boxes and sacks and loading them on to sledges. A man driving a caterpillar tractor was hauling the sledges down the slope towards a makeshift dock about fifty yards from the building. Alongside the dock the superstructure of a large submarine was visible. Nearby stood the Professor's helicopter.

Mr Pumpkinshaw said, "I bet this is where he stores the quintillium ready to send on by submarine to his secret research laboratories."

"He's planning to make something nasty with that stuff," said the Cook.

"I looked it up," said Mr Pumpkinshaw. "A chemical compound of unusual and unpredictable properties, not as yet completely analysed because of its extreme rarity, but thought to be dangerously unstable, volatile, and probably radioactive—"

"All right, all right," said the Captain irritably. "No need to go on about it."

"—and if it gets overheated it does something else," Mr Pumpkinshaw finished, "but I can't remember what."

"I'm blowed if I know how it didn't catch fire with that dratted animal sitting on it," said Captain Rumbold. "He must have damped it down with steam."

By this time we were only a quarter of a mile from the spot where the Professor stood directing his men. Warned by some sixth sense, he turned towards the sea, and caught sight of us. At the same moment, Murdo, who had been

concentrating only on the smell of the quintillium, recognized his old enemy, the Professor. Professor Shadow started back in alarm. He knew well what to expect after his earlier treatment of Murdo. He ran, screaming with fear, for the shelter of the building.

We were racing through the water at a tremendous speed towards the edge of the iceberg. We clutched the sides of our boats, too scared to do anything.

Luckily the Captain had kept his wits about him. "Make ready to let go the lines!" he shouted. Our men sprang into action, and the lines fell back loose into the water. Not a moment too soon – even as we let go, Murdo banked sharply. He tore across the sky at the Professor like a fighter plane, shooting flames from his nostrils, and fire licked instantly along the roof of the building. But the Professor was already safely inside with the door shut. The Professor's men, after a stunned look at Murdo, dropped their boxes and ran towards the dock, following the tractor with the sledges. Some of the boxes, which had been stacked round the door of the building, began to smoulder.

"My word," said the Captain, standing up in the stern of our boat to get a better view, "just look at that. Row a bit closer, boys." The crews of the lifeboats obeyed him mechanically, unable to believe their eyes.

One of the smouldering boxes was burning properly; one by one the others caught fire too. At first there was a lot of thick brown smoke, and when that cleared away we saw an intense blue flame which mounted higher and higher. It spread from box to box all around the building, travelled along the path, and surrounded the dock, the submarine, and the parked helicopter, until the entire area shimmered blue. The flames from the roof of the building joined it. It was just like the burning brandy on a plum pudding at Christmas, only three storeys high. The Professor's men ran in all directions, and some escaped. But some were engulfed by the blue fire, and fell in their tracks, burning blue themselves.

The boats stopped dead. The men had given up pulling on the oars altogether. Rocking quietly in the water, nobody uttering a word, we watched the steel doors of the building melt and a crack split the roof. We could see its outlines through the flames, and could hear the screams and shouts of the men running towards the submarine. The only other sound was Murdo's snorts as he circled above the dockside. He rushed over the cliffs of ice beyond it, flailing his wings. The fire of course had no effect on him; it rolled away like water off a duck's back.

But now the building was not only collapsing, it was turning glassy-looking. We could see the snowy ravines of the iceberg through it. Then it vanished: it was simply no longer there. Neither was the Professor. Instead, there was an immense black hole. Bit by bit the hole spread, a blot of inky blackness. It got deeper and wider. The snow round its edges crumbled, fell in, and became part of it. The hole crept along the path and swallowed the blazing crates, the tractor, and the bodies of the Professor's men. As it approached the dock, the ice-cliffs tore apart from each other in half-transparent splinters and disappeared. Then the submarine and the burning helicopter vanished into the black space. More snow and ice fell into it, and the more it devoured, the bigger and faster it grew. It began to spread in our direction.

Mr Pumpkinshaw yelled, "It's coming to get us!" We woke abruptly from our stupor; the men seized their oars and rowed like mad for the open sea. Only Captain Rumbold still gazed spellbound at the scene on the iceberg. Then he slowly removed his hat and held it over his heart.

He said solemnly, "The Professor wanted power over the whole world. With that quintillium he could have held entire countries to ransom, but in the end he has got what he deserved. It's a pity in a way. I was looking forward to clapping him into irons."

The hole was coming nearer and faster every minute, and the sweat ran down the faces of our men as they rowed away from it. Now we understood why the Professor had been so anxious to get the quintillium; as the Captain had said, he could have made himself the ruler of the world with it. Burned to ashes and atomised to nothing, he had gone for ever, the victim of his own greed.

A good deal of the iceberg by this time had been eaten by the black hole, but still a ridge half a mile long remained in the sea. Some of the survivors were stumbling along it carrying their guns. If Murdo swooped round again and tried to land there, he would run into a hail of their bullets. I screamed his name at the top of my voice and waved the biscuit tin, and the men whistled and shouted too.

At last we saw him flapping across the sky. He plunged through the blue fire, glimpsed us, and soared over our heads. Then he flopped down on top of us amidships, rocking the boat wildly, and we cheered. But our voices were hoarse and weak; we were hungry and worn out, and dreadfully shaken by the Professor's appalling fate. Murdo was exhausted too; when he had eaten what was left of the biscuits, he fell asleep across the oars, and the crew had

trouble pulling them out from under him. Under his weight, the boat went much slower, and the hole advanced on us.

Then we heard the sound of a helicopter. For a few minutes we thought it might belong to the Professor and was coming to machine-gun us, and the men began to panic. But as it flew overhead we saw Mr Dunkem leaning out of it, waving. It flew on, and landed on the dwindling iceberg. The Professor's men opened fire on it. From its markings, and the uniforms of its crew, we knew it must be one of the rescue aircraft which had been searching for us. Mr Dunkem must have got the cargo ship's captain to summon it, and had come himself to our aid. The helicopter crew sprang out of the doors, threw themselves down on their stomachs in the snow, and returned the hijackers' fire. Captain Rumbold watched through his binoculars.

"They're blazing away at each other," he said. "Keep this boat still, can't you? I can't see. Now the Professor's boys are trying to get close to the chopper. They're trying to capture it. They're putting up a thumping good fight. Ah – they're having to retreat – running out of ammunition. You can see them dodging back behind the lumps of ice and the snowdrifts." Then he fell silent.

"Go on, Captain," I said. "What's going on now?"

"It's the hole," replied Captain Rumbold slowly. "It's creeping up behind them. They've just seen it. They've retreated to the last bit of the iceberg. The hole is only twenty yards behind them – now it's fifteen – ten. Oh dear."

The sound of shooting stopped.

"Sensible fellows," said the Captain. "They are throwing

down their weapons. They're surrendering. The Navy fellows are tying them up and putting them in the chopper." He sat down on the stern-seat and wiped his face with his handkerchief. I took the binoculars from his other hand and trained them on the last of the iceberg.

Even as the chopper lifted off and swung away, the hole gobbled up the ridge of ice where it had been standing, and, a moment later, the iceberg had gone completely.

Now the hole was more than a mile wide. The sea which had surrounded the iceberg was pouring into the hole. Our men rowed on in spite of their weariness; there was now only a few hundred yards between us and it. The cargo ship was still nearly two miles away.

A shadow passed over us, and the water was fanned flat by the rotors of the naval helicopter. From its open door Mr Dunkem descended into our boat on the end of a cable. He shook hands with the Captain.

"Bit slow, weren't you, Dunkem?" said Captain Rumbold. But it was clear that he was pleased to see Mr Dunkem.

"I telegraphed the rescue services from the cargo ship," said Mr Dunkem. "They had given up looking for us, and I had a job explaining things to them. But they turned back, and we soon spotted the iceberg on the radar. Now the

chopper pilot wants us to hook the bow-lines on to his cable, and he'll tow you over to the ship – that is, if it suits you, Captain."

"Suits me down to the ground," said the Captain gruffly. "Just be quick, Dunkem, that's all."

"What's going to happen to Murdo?" I said.

"We can't get him into the chopper," said Mr Dunkem. "For one thing, it's jammed with the prisoners. We'll load him straight on to the cargo ship. We were hoping to take the quintillium off the iceberg as well, but it all seems to

have gone down that hole."

"I know," said Captain Rumbold, "and a good thing too, even if it was valuable. It's the kind of cargo I never want to see again. I don't care how useful it is to mankind."

As the Captain spoke, Mr Pumpkinshaw pointed excitedly astern. The hole no longer seemed so close behind us. In fact, it had stopped spreading. The men paused from rowing to watch it, and we waited in a breathless silence. Now it was shrinking. The sea stopped tumbling into it, and its sides began to meet together, as though it had just swallowed a huge meal and was closing its mouth. Smaller and smaller it grew, soon there was just a thin black trench in the sea, overhung by a blue haze; at last there was no sign of it at all. There were only a few lumps of quintillium lying around our feet in the boat to show that there had ever been any danger.

"There's a bit left on the floorboards, sir," said the Cook. He always hated to waste anything.

"Throw it over the side," said the Captain.

"Can't we keep just a bit for Murdo to guard?" I begged.

"Well, all right," said Captain Rumbold. "But tell him to be very careful with it."

I scraped the last of the quintillium up and (except for one small piece which I put in the biscuit tin) I threw it into the water. As we watched it sink, we thought of the vast fortune we might have had if we had got it to port; but at heart we were relieved to see it go to the bottom of the sea. We knew we were lucky it had not taken us with it.

The Northumbrian Trader, Mr Dunkem told us, as we made our lines fast to the helicopter cable, was on her way to England, escorted by a tug and manned by another crew. We were to follow on the cargo ship. It only took an hour to reach her. Murdo and I were lifted on to the deck in a net together. We were given dry clothes by the ship's crew, and their cook made us a big dinner, with steak and potatoes and treacle pudding. Murdo was given a second helping of everything, and after the dishes were cleared away, he performed some of his tricks, and made the tea kettle boil by breathing on it.

The next morning the cargo ship's radio officer brought us a message he had received from the shipping company. It congratulated us all, apologized for the inconvenience we had undergone, and promised us a reward for our courageous conduct. My share would be enough to repair my mother's house and buy her a fur coat, even though I had been a stowaway. Murdo and I would not need to go to Canada; the shipping company were so impressed by reports of his welding work that they were going to offer him a job in their shipyard. Mr Dunkem and Mr Pumpkinshaw were to be promoted. The Cook was to get enough money to open a fish and chip shop, which had always been his ambition. As for the Captain, he would get not only his full pension and a gold watch, he was to get a barometer too, and free travel on the company's ships wherever he wanted to go for the rest of his life.

We landed on the dock and the television cameras took our pictures. Reporters and harbour officials crowded round us. The Captain, turning even redder than usual, whispered to me, "Graham, who is that fine-looking woman over there waving at you?"

It was my mother. Her hair had gone grey and she was crying, but I gave her a big hug and introduced her to Captain Rumbold. He put his hat under his arm and bowed, and muttered something about how pleased he was to meet the mother of such a brave boy. My mother's tears dried at once, she went quite pink, and was too shy to do anything but stroke Murdo's head and give him a sweet from her bag.

After we had been interviewed by the television reporters, and had our hands shaken and our backs patted by a lot of people we didn't know, we were conducted to the shipping company's office in the dockside warehouse for a cup of tea. The whole crew of the Trader crowded in, and sat on the stools and desks and windowsills. Captain Rumbold found a proper chair for my mother, while the company chairman himself passed her the sugar.

The chairman held out a small flask to the Captain, and said, "Want something a little stronger in yours, Rumbold?"

The Captain was stirring his empty cup with a spoon, and gazing at my mother in an absent-minded way. He did not answer. The chairman gave him a funny look while Mr Dunkem, politely trying not to laugh, choked on his tea so that Mr Pumpkinshaw had to slap him on the back. Then the chairman, raising his voice, announced that he was giving us a holiday before the next voyage, and that he had hired a bus to take us to our homes. It turned out that Captain Rumbold was going in the same direction as we were.

What with one thing and another, not many weeks passed before Captain Rumbold mentioned to my mother that he was soon to retire from active service and was thinking of buying a nice little place in the country, not too far from the sea. He hoped that she would share it with him, of course bringing me, and Murdo too. Murdo would be able to fly to work at the shipyard every day, coming home in the evenings to be with us and to sit on his bit of quintillium. She said yes. We lost no time in making all the arrangements, getting a marriage licence, buying a ring, and booking the church. Then on a fine Saturday morning, we had the wedding. I gave my mother away, Mr Dunkem was the best man; the Cook and the rest of the Trader's crew made a grand arch of crossed oars at the church door for the bridal procession to pass beneath.

Things went quite well, except that Murdo who had never been in a church before became rather too excited. I poured some water from the font over him to cool him down, but it wasn't nearly enough. When we followed my mother and Captain Rumbold under the arch of oars, Murdo could not restrain himself any longer. In an effort to show how much he was enjoying the wedding, he sighed, and blasted my mother's hat off. As it fell to the ground and burst into flames, the Captain, in exasperation, hit Murdo over the head with his sheathed sword.

After that Murdo behaved much better, and was allowed to come with us to the reception. This took place at a hotel near the church. The Cook had made an enormous wedding cake in the form of the Northumbrian Trader with a sugar dragon on top, and it was so big that we all got three slices. Then we raised our glasses in a toast to the health of our Captain and his bride.

The Captain made a speech of thanks.

"Ladies, gentlemen, Ship's Company, distinguished guests," he said. "I've had a long career at sea, but I've never had a trip to beat this last one. But there's a lot to be grateful for, such as the cargo ship and the helicopter crews coming to our aid so promptly, and the fine seamanship of the Trader's men. All the same, I'm surprised to be standing here alive. If it wasn't for this crack-brained – I mean this amazing dragon, and this resourceful boy – we would be feeding the fishes at the bottom of the black hole. The piece of quintillium left over has been sealed in a special container and Murdo will be in charge of it from now on." We whistled and stamped our feet and cheered. The Captain held up his hand for silence, then went on, "As a rule, I don't care for boys keeping pets, but there's not much I can do about it, and anyway you'll be glad to know that my stepson Graham has undertaken to help me build a fireproof garage for Murdo behind our new house. He will also save up his pocket money and buy Mrs Rumbold a new hat. Thank you."

The Captain bowed and sat down, and we applauded him till the palms of our hands hurt.

Mr Pumpkinshaw, who had spent his reward money on a new camera, took a photograph of the whole gathering. My mother had forgiven Murdo for spoiling her hat, and she made him stand next to her in the picture. Unfortunately, Murdo was overcome with emotion; he heaved a deep sigh of happiness just as Mr Pumpkinshaw pressed the shutter, and the resulting wave of heat over-exposed the film. But we keep the foggy picture in a silver frame on our mantelpiece, and whenever I have bad dreams about Professor Shadow's swordstick, and the blue fire, and the giant black hole, I run downstairs to look at it, to remind myself of my good friends and shipmates, and of how with Murdo's help we survived the dangers of our voyage together.